Fatherhood

Insight & Wisdom from Great American Fathers

Kathryn McCabe, Contributing Editor

TRIUMPH
BOOKS
CHICAGO

2002

Dear Duff,
Happy Easter! Yet another first..... our first Easter!

I hope you enjoy this book—

I Love you sweetheart!
XOXO
Ellen

This book is available in quantity at special discounts for your group or organization. For more information, contact:

Triumph Books
601 South LaSalle Street
Chicago, Illinois 60605
(312) 939-3330 FAX (312) 663-3557

*American Heritage is a registered trademark of Forbes Inc.
Its use is pursuant to a license agreement with Forbes Inc.*

Book and jacket design by James Baran.

Printed in the United States of America.

Contents

Memories of
My Father

I learned from the example of my father that the manner in which one endures what must be endured is more important than the thing that must be endured.

— Dean Acheson

My prescription for success is based on something my father always used to tell me:
you should never try to be better than someone else,
but you should never cease trying to be the best that you can be.

— John Wooden

My father gave me a trumpet
because he loved my mother so much.

— Miles Davis

I never put aside
the past resentment of the boy
until, with my own sons, I shared
his final hours, and came to see
what he'd become, or always was—
the father who will never cease to be
alive in me.

— Jimmy Carter

[M]y father] taught me that the most powerful
weapon you have is your mind.

— Andrew Young

My success meant to [my father] everything he had worked for and believed in was true; that in America, with hard work and determination a man can achieve anything.

— Richard Nixon

I don't mind looking into the mirror and seeing my father.

— Michael Douglas

His heritage to his children wasn't words or possessions,
but an unspoken treasure, the treasure of his example
as a man and a father. More than anything I have,
I'm trying to pass that on to my children.

— Will Rogers Jr.

Papa believed the greatest sin of which we were capable
was to go to bed at night as ignorant as we had been
when we wakened that day.

— Leo Buscaglia

My father taught me to work; he did not teach me to love it.

— Abraham Lincoln

I actively opposed ways of life my country was establishing, and my father before me, and his father before him.

— Charles Lindbergh

I talk and talk and talk, and I haven't taught people in fifty years what my father taught me by example in one week.

— Mario Cuomo

♦ ♦ ♦ My father began to exercise a profound influence on me, the way religion affects some people.

— Thomas Watson Jr.

'Religion,' my father once observed to me, 'is a matter which every [person] must settle for himself.'

— Wyatt Earp

The man my brother knew as a father was not the same one I'd known. People change—even fathers.

— Leo Buscaglia

I know that moment when you go in to apologize to your kid and you end up hectoring him. I've known that as a father, and I've known that as a son.

— Harrison Ford

If I had one wish for something that would give me personal joy and satisfaction, it would be to have my father come back and show him around.
I'd like to show him the whole shooting match.

— Ted Turner

Knights in shining armor . . .
Fathers in shining trousers . . . there's little difference . . .
As they march away to work each workday.

— Paul Harvey

Observations
on Parenting

Nothing you do for children is ever wasted.
They seem not to notice us, hovering, averting our eyes,
and they seldom offer thanks,
but what we do for them is never wasted.

— Garrison Keillor

Raising kids is part joy and part guerrilla warfare.

— Edward Asner

In spite of the six thousand manuals on child raising
in the bookstores, child raising is still a dark continent and
no one really knows anything. You just need a lot of love
and luck—and, of course, courage.

— Bill Cosby

There are only two lasting bequests we can hope to give our children. One of these is roots; the other, wings.

— Hodding Carter

Everyone likes to think that he has done reasonably well in life, so that it comes as a shock to find out our children believing differently. The temptation is to tune them out; it takes much more courage to listen.

— John D. Rockefeller III

Parenthood remains the greatest single preserve
of the amateur.

— Alvin Toffler

Being a parent is not something that people ever feel
confident or secure about.

— Garrison Keillor

What the best and wisest parent wants for his own child, that
must be what the community wants for all its children.

— John Dewey

Human beings are the only creatures
that allow their children to come back home.

— Bill Cosby

• • • Parenting never ends.

— Bob Keeshan (Captain Kangaroo)

Love is the chain whereby to bind a child to his parents.

— Abraham Lincoln

It is our continuing love for our children
that makes us want them to become all they can be,
and their continuing love for us helps them accept healthy
discipline—from us and eventually from themselves.

— Fred Rogers (Mr. Rogers)

◆ ◆ ◆ What you do for yourselves and for your children
can never be taken away.

— Robert Kennedy

Observations on Children and Childhood

All kids need is a little help, a little hope,
and somebody who believes in them.

— Earvin (Magic) Johnson

That energy which makes a child hard to manage
is the energy which afterward makes him a manager of life.

— Henry Ward Beecher

♦ ♦ ♦ the most used word in a child's dictionary is 'why?'

— Steven Spielberg

Water fascinates kids. They run toward it,
and they run away from it. They love it in a lake or an ocean,
but it's a necessary evil in a bathtub.

— Art Linkletter

This would be a better world for children
if parents had to eat the spinach.

— Groucho Marx

There's a time—all too brief
as it too soon becomes apparent to parents—
to be little; a time to be in between; and a time to be old.
Let each have its season. Let little be little.

— Malcolm Forbes

We mold the views of our children
from their earliest days in many ways, some open, some subtle.
Long after they are gone from the home these views remain
with them, some as haunting as a demon.

— Bob Keeshan (Captain Kangaroo)

There isn't a child who hasn't gone out into the brave new
world who eventually doesn't return to the old homestead
carrying a bundle of dirty clothes.

— Art Buchwald

Adolescence is that period in a kid's life
when his or her parents become more difficult.

— Ryan O'Neal

All my children have spoken for themselves since they first learned to speak and not always with my advance approval and I expect that to continue in the future.

— Gerald Ford

A child doesn't blindly accept things as they are, doesn't blindly believe in limits, doesn't blindly believe in the words spoken by some authority figure like me.

— Steven Spielberg

Childhood is frequently a solemn business for those inside it.

— George F. Will

I have learned that my kids, like most kids,
would rather work all night long in a salt mine
than rake leaves at home.

— Phil Donahue

Children are not our creations but our guests.

— John Updike

A child's spirit is like a child,
you can never catch it by running after it;
you must stand still, and, for love,
it will soon itself come back.

— Arthur Miller

The Importance of Children

The Importance of Children

A person's a person no matter how small.

— Theodor Geisel (Dr. Seuss)

Youth comes but once in a lifetime.

— Henry Wadsworth Longfellow

Fortunately for us and our world, youth is not easily
discouraged. Youth with its clear vista and boundless faith and
optimism is uninhibited by the thousands of considerations that
always bedevil man in his progress. The hopes of the world rest
on the flexibility, vigor, capacity for new thought,
the fresh outlook of the young.

— Dwight D. Eisenhower

We will die without our young people.

— Alex Haley

If all the world thought and acted like children, we'd never have any trouble. The only pity is even kids have to grow up.

— Walt Disney

Each child is an adventure into a better life— an opportunity to change the old pattern and make it new.

— Hubert H. Humphrey

Really give yourself to your children
just as your parents gave themselves to you
because they are the future of your generation.

— Ross Perot

It is easier to build strong children than to repair broken men.

— Frederick Douglass

A child miseducated is a child lost.

— John F. Kennedy

I confess pride in the coming generation.
You are working out your own salvation;
you are more in love with life;
you play with fire openly, where we did in secret,
and few of you are burned.

— Franklin D. Roosevelt

Children are a great investment.
They beat the hell out of stocks.

— Peter Lynch

The Importance of Children

If youth is a defect, it is one that we outgrow too soon.

— Robert Lowell

Adults are obsolete children.

— Theodor Geisel (Dr. Seuss)

The reconstruction of children is more precious than factories and bridges.

— Herbert Hoover

Youth is the turning point of life,
the most sensitive and volatile period, the state that registers
most vividly the impressions and experience of life.

— Richard Wright

A torn jacket is soon mended,
but hard words bruise the heart of a child.

— Henry Wadsworth Longfellow

Children are our most valuable natural resource.

— Herbert Hoover

We find delight in the beauty and happiness of children
that makes the heart too big for the body.

— Ralph Waldo Emerson

A child is a person who is going to carry on what you have
started . . . that fate of humanity is in his hands.

— Abraham Lincoln

Children and dogs are as necessary
to the welfare of this country
as Wall Street and the railroads.

— Harry S. Truman

Young children are not all that different
from the adults they will become.

— Bob Keeshan (Captain Kangaroo)

Family First

A man's rootage is more important than his leafage.

— Woodrow Wilson

As much as I converse with sages and heroes,
they have very little of my love and admiration.
I long for rural and domestic scenes, for the warbling
of birds and the prattling of my children.

— John Adams

The only rock I know that stays steady,
the only institution I know that works, is the family.

— Lee Iacocca

The happiest moments of my life have been the few which I have passed at home in the bosom of my family.

— Thomas Jefferson

Acting is just a way of making a living, the family is life.

— Denzel Washington

Never come between blood and blood.

— Clint Eastwood

For unflagging interest and enjoyment,
a household of children, if things go reasonably well, certainly
makes all other forms of success and achievement
lose their importance by comparison.

— Theodore Roosevelt

I'm still not sure what is meant by good fortune and success. I
know fame and power are for the birds. But then life suddenly
comes into focus for me. And, ah, there stand my kids.

— Lee Iacocca

The happiness of the domestic fireside
is the first boon of mankind . . .

— Thomas Jefferson

. . . fond as I am of the White House
and much though I have appreciated these years in it,
there isn't any place in the world like home . . .

— Theodore Roosevelt

. . . We may find some of our best friends in our own blood.

— Ralph Waldo Emerson

No one on his deathbed ever said,
'I wish I had spent more time on my business.'

— Paul Tsongas

You may be a pain in the ass, you may be bad,
but child, you belong to me.

— Ray Charles

Home
and Family

Family life is the basis for a strong community and a great nation.

— Bing Crosby

Homesick is a queer word as we use it sometimes when what we really mean is that we would like to be in two places at the same time. And so we are trying to live more of life than can be lived in one place at a certain time.

— Carl Sandburg

In our family, we try to make something happen rather than wait around for it to happen.

— James Jordan

[In a big family] the first child is kind of like the first pancake. If it's not perfect, that's okay, there are a lot more coming along.

— Antonin Scalia

I was the seventh of nine children, and when you come from that far down you have to struggle to survive.

— Robert Kennedy

When you're the only pea in the pod,
your parents are likely to get you confused with
the Hope diamond.

— Russell Baker

Always obey your parents, when they are present.

— Mark Twain

I'm not the audience; I'm the dad.

— Stephen Stills

Home is the sanctuary where the healing is . . .

— Walter Cronkite

Home is the place there's no place like.

— Charles Schulz

There is nothing emptier than a house
once occupied by a wife and five children . . .

— Phil Donahue

Families break up when people take hints you don't intend
and miss hints you do intend.

— Robert Frost

The point I want to make to you is, role models can be black.
Role models can be white. Role models can be generals.
Role models can be principals, teachers, doctors,
or just your parent who brought you into this world
and who is trying to give you the best of everything.

— General Colin Powell

Hopes
and Fears

May you build a ladder to the stars and climb on every rung.
And, may you stay forever young.

— Bob Dylan

I have a dream . . . that my four little children will one day live
in a nation where they will not be judged by the color of their
skin but by the content of their character.

— Martin Luther King Jr.

My hope for my children must be that they respond to the
still, small voice of God in their own hearts.

— Andrew Young

When we leave our child in nursery school for the first time, it won't be just our child's feelings about separation that we will have to cope with, but our own feelings as well—from our present and from our past, parents are extra vulnerable to new tremors from old earthquakes.

— Fred Rogers (Mr. Rogers)

One parent or the other got up late in the night to come in and see if your backside was moving up and down.

— Garrison Keillor

If there must be trouble let it be in my day, that my child may have peace.

— Thomas Paine

How do you explain to a little child
why you have to go to jail?

— Martin Luther King Jr.

♦ ♦ ♦ We all fear the unknown—the strange, the different.
The natural fears of parents are made worse by ignorance,
and unfortunately, they pass them down to their children.

— Jackie Robinson

I know there is no good in my trying to explain to you
why I am away from home—war doesn't make any sense
even when you are grown up.

— (Lieutenant) Henry Fonda

One of the most painful experiences I have ever faced
was to see [my daughter's] tears when I told her
that Funtown was closed to colored children . . .
for at that moment the first dark cloud . . . had floated
into her little mental sky.

— Martin Luther King Jr.

The Journey
of Life

I would like you to be a defiant little point of light
at the end of a diamond, and if you have fools to be with,
to make them a setting.

— F. Scott Fitzgerald

You'll make a lot of mistakes in your life . . . but if you learn
from every mistake, you really didn't make a mistake.

— Vince Lombardi

In the really important decisions of life, others cannot help
you. No matter how much they would like to. You must rely
only on yourself. That is the fate of each one of us.

— Eugene O'Neill

♦ ♦ ♦ Sometimes people can be funny. They'll turn on you
when you're a star.

— James Jordan

Son, you get out of it what you put into it.

— Earl Woods

You don't want to do what I'm doing.

— Vince Lombardi

As you journey through [life], you will encounter all sorts of these nasty little upsets, and you will either learn to adjust yourself to them or gradually go nuts.

— Groucho Marx

Son, sometimes no action is action. The army that marches forward is not always the one that wins.

— Ellis Marsalis

It is while we are young that the habit of industry is formed. If not then, it never is afterwards. The fortune of our lives, therefore, depends on employing well the short period of youth.

— Thomas Jefferson

All I believe in in life is the rewards for virtue (according to your talents) and the punishments for not fulfilling your duties, which are doubly costly.

— F. Scott Fitzgerald

You can make it. It gets dark sometimes, but the morning comes. Don't you surrender. Suffering breeds character. Character breeds faith. In the end, faith will not disappoint.

— Jesse Jackson

After all, parents' advice is no damned good. You know that as well as I. The best I can do is try to encourage you to work hard at something you really want to do and have the ability to do.

— Eugene O'Neill

• • • $n$ever follow anybody who's working less than you.

— Ellis Marsalis

You have everything to live for.
Put yourself in condition to live.

— William Randolph Hearst

Parenting
a Newborn

When you're drawing up your list of life's miracles, you might place near the top the first moment your baby smiles at you.

— Bob Greene

There are one hundred and fifty-two distinctly different ways of holding a baby—and all are right.

— Heywood C. Broun

I felt something impossible for me to explain in words. Then when they took her away, it hit me. I got scared all over again and began to feel giddy. Then it came to me—I was a father.

— Nat King Cole

Never will a time come when the most marvelous recent invention is as marvelous as a newborn baby.

— Carl Sandburg

Babies are always more trouble than you thought— and more wonderful.

— Charles Osgood

Infancy is the perpetual Messiah, which comes into the arms of fallen men, and pleads with them to return to paradise.

— Ralph Waldo Emerson

A baby is God's opinion that life should go on.

— Carl Sandburg

I love to think that the day you're born,
you're given the world as a birthday present.

— Leo Buscaglia

Mrs. Monroe hath added a daughter to our society
who tho' noisy, contributes greatly to its amusement.

— James Monroe

Taking care of a newborn baby means devoting yourself,
body and soul, twenty-four hours a day, seven days a week,
to the welfare of someone whose major response, in the
way of positive reinforcement, is to throw up on you.

— Dave Barry

Infancy conforms to nobody; all conform to it.

— Ralph Waldo Emerson

. . . nothing gets you ready for that first night
when you're out of the hospital and alone, and she's crying
and won't stop and you're holding her against you
while her screams rock your chest.

— Bob Greene

The first cry of a newborn baby in Chicago or Zamboango,
in Amsterdam or Rangoon, has the same pitch and key,
each saying 'I am! I have come through! I belong!'

— Carl Sandburg

Fathers and Daughters

It wasn't until she was two
and realized she was stuck with me that she said,
during a walk through autumn leaves, 'I love you . . .'

— James Thurber

She entered the world with a commanding voice
and has been taking over ever since.

— Lyndon Johnson

It isn't that I'm a weak father,
it's just that she's a strong daughter.

— Henry Fonda

Mary Ellin, Mary Ellin
Is her Daddy's girl.
It must be understood
Only when she is good
Is Mary Ellin, Mary Ellin
Her Daddy's girl.

— Irving Berlin

She is my life.

— Gary Cooper

Do you want to know how you can be so beautiful and sweet?
It is easy. Only try with all your resolution, to mind what that
silent teacher in your breast says to you . . .

— Bronson Alcott

Past experience indicates that the best way of dealing with her is total attention and love.

— Lyndon Johnson

Then farewell, my dear;
my loved daughter adieu;
the last pang of life is in parting from you.

— Thomas Jefferson

The meaningful role of the father of the bride was played out long before the church music began. It stretched across those years of infancy and puberty, adolescence and young adulthood. That's when she needs you at her side.

— Tom Brokaw

When you were a few weeks old, you smiled on us.
I sometimes see the same look and the same smile on your face,
and feel that my daughter is yet good and pure. O keep it
there, my daughter, and never lose it.

— Bronson Alcott

The other night, my little teen-age daughter came home and
said—and I don't think she was being very original—
'Daddy, as an outsider, how do you feel about the human race?'

— Lyndon Johnson

Fathers
and Sons

The father is always a Republican toward his son,
and his mother's always a Democrat.

— Robert Frost

A boy has two jobs. One is just being a boy.
The other is growing up to be a man.

— Herbert Hoover

A boy wants something very special from his father.
You hear it said that fathers want their sons to be what
they feel they cannot themselves be,
but I tell you it also works the other way.

— Sherwood Anderson

You don't raise heroes, you raise sons.
And if you treat them like sons, they'll turn out to be heroes,
even if it's just in your own eyes.

— Walter Schirra Sr.

And as I hung up the phone it occurred to me,
he'd grown up just like me.
My boy was just like me.

— Harry Chapin

The problem is I like him too much and he knows it.

— Bobby Knight

◆ ◆ ◆ little girls are in fact smaller versions of real human
beings, whereas little boys are Pod People
from the Planet Destructo.

— Dave Barry

A father follows the course of his son's life and notes many
things of which he has not the privilege to speak.
He sees, of course, his own past life unfolding . . .

— William Carlos Williams

Every son, at one point or another, defies his father,
fights him, departs from him, only to return to him—if he is
lucky—closer and more secure than before.

— Leonard Bernstein

Build me a son, O Lord,
who will be strong enough to know when he is weak,
and brave enough to face himself when he is afraid;
one who will be proud and unbending in honest defeat,
and humble and gentle in victory.

— General Douglas MacArthur

The Joys
of Parenting

Children make you want to start life over.

— Muhammad Ali

A father's interest in having a child—perhaps his only child—may be unmatched by any other interest in his life.

— William Rehnquist

Parents are like shuttles on a loom. They join the threads of the past with threads of the future and leave their own bright patterns as they go.

— Fred Rogers (Mr. Rogers)

There is no friendship, no love,
like that of the parent for the child.

— Henry Ward Beecher

We are given children to test us and make us more spiritual.

— George F. Will

If you are the first child, you are one of two most amazing things that happened to your parents. A couple. And if you came later in the family, you were just as amazing as that, but without all of the worry and the facts.

— Garrison Keillor

♦ ♦ ♦ You will judge yourself by how your children turn out.

— Ross Perot

When you become a parent it is your biggest chance to grow again. You have another crack at yourself.

— Fred Rogers (Mr. Rogers)

Fatherhood is responsibility, it's definitely humility,
a lot of love and the friendships of a parent and child.

— Denzel Washington

By profession I am a soldier and take pride in that fact.
But I am prouder—infinitely prouder—to be a father.

— General Douglas MacArthur

We receive our pay from you as we go, tenfold.
Confidence is a plant of slow growth,
but in your case, it was a sturdy plant long years ago.

— John D. Rockefeller Sr.

Every one of your letters I read first for the facts and the fun—and then a second time to see how the red inside heart of you is ticking.

— Carl Sandburg

When I was a young man before I had children, I was a sad man.

— Garrison Keillor

I'm really profoundly proud and fond of you—
after my fashion which is inarticulate about such things—
and I know there is a rare feeling between us that
ought to make both of our lives richer as years go by.

— Eugene O'Neill

I feel blessed, but quite frankly, . . . I used to say 'Why me,
Lord? What have I done to deserve this beautiful
and special kid?'

— Earl Woods

He makes fuzz come out of my bald patch!

— Charles Lindbergh

The Joys of
Grandparenting

Nobody can do for little children what grandparents do.
Grandparents sort of sprinkle stardust
over the lives of little children.

— Alex Haley

There is nothing like having grandchildren
to restore your faith in heredity.

— Doug Larson

Because [grandparents] are usually free to love and guide and
befriend the young without having to take daily responsibility
for them, they can often reach out past pride and fear of failure
and close the space between generations.

— Jimmy Carter

Few things seem more satisfying than seeing
your children have teenagers of their own.

— Doug Larson

Grandparents are our continuing tie to the near-past,
to the events and beliefs and experiences that so strongly
affect our lives and the world around us.

— Jimmy Carter

Declarations

Youth are looking for something; it's up to adults
to show them what is worth emulating.

— Jesse Jackson

We cannot always build the future for our youth,
but we can build our youth for the future.

— Franklin D. Roosevelt

Make a world worthy of the children
your generation will bear.

— Carl Sagan

Learn about your family. Find out about your grandmother's grandfather. Where was he in 1861? It will help you, I promise.

— Ken Burns

Your parents left you a perfect world. Don't louse it up.

— Art Buchwald

Anybody who is in a position to discipline others should first learn to accept discipline himself.

— Malcolm X

Discipline itself must be disciplined.

— M. Scott Peck

If you take care of yourself and your family and provide that one unit of well-being in the world, you'll have done your part.

— Andy Rooney

We have for a full lifetime taught our children to be go-getters. Can we now say to them that if they want to be happy, they must be go-givers?

— Mario Cuomo

Every adult is a teacher to every child.

— Dan Rather

Millions of Americans,
especially our own sons and daughters,
are seeking a cause they can believe in.
There is a hunger in the country today—
a hunger for spiritual guidance.

— Ronald Reagan

If I were given the opportunity to present a gift
to the next generation, it would be the ability for each
individual to learn to laugh at himself.

— Charles Schulz

If the very old will remember, the very young will listen.

— Chief Dan George

Once you bring life into the world, you must protect it.
We must protect it by changing the world.

— Elie Wiesel

I want you to create families and raise children who are God-fearing, who are loving, who are clean, and who are determined to do even better than their parents.

— General Colin Powell

Do not neglect your work, but start families. Make babies, lots of them. Say twenty-five.

— Ken Burns

If men do not keep on speaking terms with children, they cease to be men, and become merely machines for eating and for earning money.

— John Updike

A Parent's Words
of Wisdom

Perhaps a child who is fussed over gets a feeling of destiny, he thinks he is in the world for something important and it gives him drive and confidence.

— Benjamin Spock

My parents were constantly affirming me in everything I did. Late at night I'd wake up and hear my mother talking over my bed, saying, 'You're going to do great on this test. You can do anything you want.'

— Stephen Covey

You need a lot of money to raise a modern child. Hair gel alone will run you thousands of dollars.

— Dave Barry

The average child is an almost non-existent myth.
To be normal one must be peculiar in some way or another.

— Heywood C. Broun

Parents who expect change in themselves
as well as in their children, who accept it
and find in it the joy as well as the pains of growth,
are likely to be the happiest and most confident parents.

— Fred Rogers (Mr. Rogers)

Like any father, I have moments when I wonder whether I
belong to my children or they belong to me.

— Bob Hope

Rediscovering fatherhood a second time,
I was finding that like youth, it is wasted on the young.

— Arthur Miller

As far as rearing children goes, the basic idea
I try to keep in mind is that a child is a person.
Just because they happen to be a little shorter than
you doesn't mean they are dumber than you.

— Frank Zappa

I have found the best way to give advice to your children is
to find out what they want and then advise them to do it.

— Harry S. Truman

As you raise your families, remember the worst kind of poverty is not economic poverty, it is the poverty of values. It is the poverty of caring. It is the poverty of love.

— General Colin Powell

We never know the love of our parent for us till we have become parents.

— Henry Ward Beecher

Some authority on parenting once said, 'Hold them very close and then let them go.' This is the hardest truth for a father to learn: that his children are continuously growing up and moving away from him . . .

— Bill Cosby

As a father of two
there is a respectful question
which I wish to ask of fathers of five:
How do you happen to be still alive?

— Ogden Nash

As our children grow, so must we grow to meet their changing
emotional, intellectual, and designer-footware needs.

— Dave Barry

Sometimes you struggle so hard to feed your family
one way, you forget to feed them the other way, with
spiritual nourishment. Everybody needs that.

— James Brown

We carry adolescence around in our bodies all our lives. We get through the Car Crash Age alive and cruise through our early twenties as cool dudes, wily, dashing, winsome . . . shooting baskets, the breeze, the moon, and then we try to become caring men, good husbands, great fathers, good citizens.

— Garrison Keillor

At its best, parenting occurs
in the spirit of equal partnership.

— Benjamin Spock

New parents quickly learn that raising children
is a kind of desperate improvisation.

— Bill Cosby

Advice on
Raising a Child

When a child can be brought to tears,
not from fear of punishment, but from repentance for his
offense, he needs no chastisement. When the tears begin to flow
from grief at one's own conduct, be sure there is an angel
nestling in the bosom.

— Horace Mann

A good father is a little bit of a mother.

— Lee Salk

Trust yourself. You know more than you think you do.

— Benjamin Spock

Re raising kids: Love, without discipline, isn't.

— Malcolm Forbes

For God Sake make your children hardy, active, and industrious, for Strength, Activity, and Industry will be their only Resource and Dependence.

— John Adams

Try to see your children as whole and complete . . . as though they are already what they can become.

— Wayne Dyer

Respect the child. Be not too much his parent.
Trespass not on his solitude.

— Ralph Waldo Emerson

What your child needs from you is mothering or fathering—
not psychologizing.

— Lee Salk

The average parent will go through the full gamut of ups and downs and trials and tribulations. The key is developing close ties with your children, teaching them to perform and function effectively.

— Earl Woods

Our only realistic hope, as I see it, is first to bring up our children with a feeling that they are in this world not for their own satisfaction but primarily to serve others.

— Benjamin Spock

Let your children go if you want to keep them.

— Malcolm Forbes

Children will send verbal and non-verbal signals
when everything is not okay.
Parents have but to listen.

— Bob Keeshan (Captain Kangaroo)

The baby whose cries are answered now will later be the child
confident enough to show his independence and curiosity.

— Lee Salk

Let thy child's first lesson be obedience,
and the second will be what thou wilt.

— Benjamin Franklin

The most important thing in the world is that you make yourself the greatest, grandest, most wonderful loving person in the world because this is what you are going to be giving to your children . . .

— Leo Buscaglia

It should be your care, therefore, and mine, to elevate the minds of our children and exalt their courage . . .

— John Adams

Your children need your presence
more than your presents.

— Jesse Jackson

Spoil your baby. During the first year give him all
the attention he wants, because this is when he is learning
to love and trust. Later, . . . these feelings become
the best basis for discipline.

— Lee Salk

Advice to Children

Try to remain humble. Smartness kills everything.

— Sherwood Anderson

Don't let me catch either of you coming back [from school] perfect in deportment!

— Charles Lindbergh

You know what makes a good loser? Practice.

— Ernest Hemingway

Son, if anyone ever calls you a nigger, you not only got my permission to fight him, you got my orders to fight him.

— Thurgood Marshall

Any boy of your age who disobeys his mother, or worries her, or is disrespectful to her—such a boy is a poor, shabby fellow; and, if you know any such boys, you ought to cut their acquaintance.

— Herman Melville

I don't want you to be a soldier or a priest but a good useful man.

— William Tecumseh Sherman

Next [in importance] to occupation is the building up of good taste. That is difficult, slow work. Few achieve it. It means all the difference in the world.

— Sherwood Anderson

Where there is no occasion for expressing an opinion, it is best to be silent . . .

— George Washington

Be smart, but never show it.

— L. B. Mayer

♦ ♦ ♦ **a** man might do some might good work and not be a
gentleman in any sense.

— Theodore Roosevelt

The only fatherly advice I have ever given you
is to not eat your peas off a knife.

— John Cheever

♦ ♦ ♦ **I**f you went abroad, you would lose one of the greatest
privileges this country gives, that is, an American education.

— W. C. Fields

You won't arrive. It is an endless search.

— Sherwood Anderson

Keep your balance, the grades don't matter.

— Robert Frost

Think the best of people, do not dwell upon their faults, [and] try not to see them. You will be happier for it.

— Mark Twain

♦ ♦ ♦ I haven't taught you anything about the value of money. Basically, it's worthless, but it lets you buy a lot of things that you can enjoy . . . We won't always have this much, so enjoy it while you can.

— Ernest Hemingway

Someday you're going to have to tell your dad to go to hell.

— Warren Buffett

It's important to be smart in school, but it's even more important to be smart about yourself.

— Irving Berlin

Advice on Love
and Marriage

Girls have a way of knowing or feeling what you feel,
but they usually like to hear it also.

— John Steinbeck

♦ ♦ ♦ love may and therefore ought to be under the guidance
of reason, for although we cannot avoid first impressions, we
may assuredly place them under guard . . .

— George Washington

You'll have many, many friends, but if your relationship
with your mate is one hundred percent of your heart,
you'll never need a friend.

— Bill Cosby

Harmony in the marriage state is the very first object
to be aimed at.

— Thomas Jefferson

The object of love is the best and most beautiful.
Try to live up to it.

— John Steinbeck

You don't have to deserve your mother's love. You have to
deserve your father's. He's more particular.

— Robert Frost

Parental love is the only real charity going. It never comes back. A one-way street.

— Abbie Hoffman

Next to God, thy parents.

— William Penn

It sometimes happens that what you feel is not returned for one reason or another—but that does not make your feeling less valuable and good.

— John Steinbeck

Advice on Success

Circumstances have nothing to do with success.
When you have made up your mind, success is certain.

— William Randolph Hearst

It isn't your success I want.
There is a possibility of your having a decent attitude
toward people and work.
That alone may make a man of you.

— Sherwood Anderson

Where creative effort is involved,
there are no trivial circumstances.
The most trivial of them may ruin the whole issue.

— Frank Lloyd Wright

He who is taught to live upon little
owes more to his father's wisdom than he who has a great deal
left him does to his father's care.

— William Penn

You must keep your mind on the objective,
not on the obstacle.

— William Randolph Hearst

The parent who leaves his son enormous wealth generally
deadens the talents and energies of the son.

— Andrew Carnegie

I'd hate to see any descendents of mine fall into the category
of what I'd call 'idle rich'—
a group I've never had much use for . . .

— Sam Walton

Wise people who save money have just as much satisfaction
out of savings as jackasses have out of spending it.

— William Randolph Hearst

Your dad will never be reckoned among the great.
But you can be sure he did his level best and gave all he had
to his country . . . What more can a person do?

— Harry S. Truman

Life Lessons

Twenty years from now you will be more disappointed by
the things you didn't do than by the ones you did do. So
throw off the bowlines. Sail away from the safe harbor.
Catch the trade winds in your sails. Explore. Dream. Discover.

— Mark Twain

My dad told me there's no difference between
a black snake and a white snake. They both bite.

— Thurgood Marshall

Honor does not descend, but ascend.

— Benjamin Franklin

◆ ◆ ◆ It is so remarkably easy just to tell the truth in this world, that I often marvel that there are so many madly foolish, so wretchedly stupid, that they hide truth.

— Jack London

Many of the lessons I learned came as a result of terrible clashes with my father.

— Thomas Watson Jr.

Our maker has given us this faithful internal Monitor, and if you always obey it, you will always be prepared for the end of the world; or for a much more certain event which is death.

— Thomas Jefferson

◆ ◆ ◆ Character counts for a great deal more
than either intellect or body in winning success in life . . .

— Theodore Roosevelt

Always remember life is not as complex
as many people would have you think.

— Thomas Watson Sr.

Life is a problem in virtual velocity.
The purpose . . . is the direction.

— William Tecumseh Sherman

. . . good name and honor are worth more than
all the gold and jewels ever mined.

— Harry S. Truman

When I was a boy of 14, my father was so ignorant,
I could hardly stand to have the old man around.
But when I got to be 21, I was astonished at how much
the old man had learned in seven years.

— Mark Twain

Index

FATHERHOOD

Sources

Adler, Bill, ed. *Presidential Wit From Washington to Johnson*. New York: Trident Press, 1996.

Albanese, Andrew and Brandon Trissler, eds. *Graduation Day*. New York: William Morrow, 1998.

Ali, Muhammad. *The Greatest*. New York: Ballantine Books, 1975.

Andrews, Robert, ed. *The Columbia Dictionary of Quotations*. New York: Columbia University Press, 1993.

Baker, Russell. *Inventing the Truth: The Art and Craft of Memoir*. Edited by William Zinsser. Boston: Houghton Mifflin, 1987.

Barrett, Mary Ellin. *Irving Berlin: A Daughter's Memoir*. New York: Simon & Schuster, 1994.

Barry, Dave. *Dave Barry Turns 40*. New York: Crown, 1990.

Bedell, Madelon. *The Alcotts: Biography of a Family*. New York: Clarkson Potter, 1980.

Beecher, Henry Ward. *Proverbs from Plymouth Pulpit*, 1887.

Bell, Janet Cheatham, ed. *The Soul of Success: Inspiring Quotations*. New York: J. Wiley, 1997.

Bennett, William J., ed. *Our Sacred Honor*. New York: Simon & Schuster, 1997.

Berg, Scott A. *Lindbergh*. New York: G.P. Putnam's, 1998.

Bernstein, Burton. *Thurber, A Biography*. New York: Dodd, Mead, 1975.

Bishop, Joseph Bucklin, ed. *Theodore Roosevelt's Letters to His Children*. New York: Scribner's, 1919.

Bohle, Bruce, ed. *The Home Book of American Quotations*. New York: Dodd, 1967.

Brallier, Jess M., ed. *Presidential Wit & Wisdom: Maxims, Mottoes, Sound Bites, Speeches, and Asides*. New York: Penguin Books, 1996.

Braude, Jacob Morton, ed. *Lifetime Speaker's Encyclopedia*. Englewood Cliffs, NJ: Prentice Hall, 1962.

Brown, James and Bruce Tucker. *The Godfather of Soul*. New York: Macmillan, 1986.

Broyard, Anatole. *Aroused by Books*. New York: Random House, 1974.

Burton, Humphrey. *Leonard Bernstein*. Garden City, NY: Doubleday, 1994.

Burns, K. "Spotlight: Denzel," *Essence* 17 (1986):54-6.

Buscaglia, Leo. *Papa, My Father: A Celebration of Dads*. Thorofare, NJ: Slack, 1989.

Butterfield, L.H., March Friedlaender, and Mary-Jo Kline, eds. *The Book of Abigail and John: Selected Letters of the Adams Family, 1762-1884*. Cambridge, MA: Harvard University Press and Massachussetts Historical Society, 1975.

Camp, Wesley D., ed. *What a Piece of Work Is Man! Camp's Unfamiliar Quotations From 2000 B.C. to the Present*. Englewood Cliffs, NJ: Prentice Hall, 1990.

Carruth, Gorton, ed. *Harper Book of American Quotations*. New York: Harper & Row, 1988.

Carter, Hodding. *Reader's Digest* (May 1953):52.

Carter, Jimmy. *Always a Reckoning and Other Poems*. Thorndike, ME: G.K. Hall, 1995.

"Celebrities recall best advice given by their fathers." *Jet* 92 (1997):56-62.

Charles, Ray and David Ritz. *Brother Ray*. New York: Warner, 1978.

Cohen, G. "The ties that bind—even today: Fathers and sons in business." *U.S. News and World Report* 109 (July 9, 1990):38.

Cosby, Bill. *Fatherhood*. Garden City, NY: Doubleday, 1986.

Davis, Merrell R. and William H. Gilman, eds. *The Letters of Herman Melville*. New Haven, CT: Yale University Press, 1960.

Donahue, Phil. *Donahue, My Own Story*. New York: Simon & Schuster, 1979.

Douglas, Charles Noel, ed. *Forty Thousand Quotations, Prose and Poetical.* New York: G. Sully and Company, 1917.

Douglas, Kirk. *The Ragman's Son.* New York: Pocket Books, 1988.

Dylan, Bob. "Forever Young," from *Bob Dylan at Budokan.* Columbia Records, 1979.

Ehrlich, Eugene and Marshall DeBruhl, eds. *International Thesaurus of Quotations.* New York: Harper Perennial, 1996.

Eisel, Deborah Davis and Jill Swanson Reddig, eds. *Dictionary of Contemporary Quotations.* John Gordan Burke Publisher, 1981.

Emerson, Ralph Waldo. "Illusions," from *The Conduct of Life,* 1860.

Emerson, Ralph Waldo. *Hitch Your Wagon to a Star.* New York: Columbia University Press, 1996.

Emerson, Ralph Waldo. *The Letters of Ralph Waldo Emerson,* volume six. Edited by Ralph L. Rusk. New York: Columbia University Press, 1939.

Ernst, Joseph W., ed. *"Dear Father/Dear Son," Correspondence of John D. Rockefeller and John D. Rockefeller Jr.* New York: Fordham University Press, 1994.

Feinstein, John. *A Season on the Brink: A Year with Bobby Knight and the Indiana Hoosiers.* New York: Simon & Schuster, 1986.

Fellman, Michael. *Citizen Sherman: A Life of William Tecumseh Sherman.* New York: Random House, 1995.

Fields, W. C. *By Himself: His Intended Autobiography.* Commentary by Ronald J. Fields. Englewood Cliffs, NJ: Prentice Hall, 1973.

Flynn, George L. *The Vince Lombardi Scrapbook.* New York: Grosset & Dunlap, 1976.

Fonda, Henry. *Fonda: My Life.* New York: New American Library, 1981.

Forbes Magazine, ed. *Thoughts on the Business of Life.* Chicago: Triumph Books, 1992.

Freeman, Criswell, ed. *Fathers Are Forever.* Nashville: Walnut Grove Press, 1998.

Frost, Elizabeth, ed. *Bully Pulpit: Quotations From America's Presidents.* New York: Facts On File, 1988.

Frost, Robert and Elinor Frost. *Family Letters of Robert and Elinor Frost.* Edited by Arnold Grade. Albany: State University of New York Press, 1972.

Ginsburg, Susan, ed. *Family Wisdom: The 2000 Most Important Things Ever Said About Parenting, Children and Family Life.* New York: Columbia University Press, 1996.

Goldberg, Robert and Gerald Jay Goldberg. *Citizen Turner.* New York: Harcourt Brace, 1995.

Goodman, Ted, ed. *Forbes Book of Business Quotations: 14,266 Thoughts on the Business of Life.* New York: Black Dog & Leventhal Publishers, 1997.

Greene, Bob. *Good Morning, Merry Sunshine: A Father's Journal of His Child's First Year.* New York: Atheneum, 1984.

Griswold, Robert L., ed. *Fatherhood in America: A History.* New York: Basic Books, 1993.

Handley, Helen and Andra Samelson, eds. *Child.* Wainscott, NY: Pushcart Press, 1988.

Harnsbinger, Caroline. *Mark Twain, Family Man.* New York: Citadel Press, 1960.

Hearst, William Randolph Jr. *The Hearsts, Father and Son.* New York: Roberts Rinehart, 1991.

Hemingway, Gregory H. *Papa: A Personal Memoir.* Boston: Houghton Mifflin, 1976.

Hill, Harold, ed. *Life Isn't Fair: 300 Years of Advice From History's Most Memorable Commencements.* New York: Berkley Publishing Group, 1997.

Hoffman, Edward. *The Book of Fathers' Wisdom: Paternal Advice from Moses to Bob Dylan.* Secaucus, NJ: Carol Publishing Group, 1998.

Sources

Iacocca, Lee and Sonny Kleinfeld. *Talking Straight.* Boston: G.K. Hall, 1988.

Jackson, Venice, ed. *Heart Full of Grace: A Thousand Years of Black Wisdom.* New York: Simon & Schuster, 1995.

Jenkins, Garry. *Harrison Ford: Imperfect Hero.* Secaucus, NJ: Carol Publishing Group, 1997.

Johnson, Magic and William Novak. *My Life.* New York: Random House, 1992.

Keeshan, Robert. *Growing Up Happy.* New York: Doubleday, 1989.

Keillor, Garrison. *The Book of Guys.* New York: Viking, 1993.

Kennedy, Robert F. *Make Gentle the Life of This World: The Vision of Robert F. Kennedy.* New York: Harcourt Brace, 1998.

King, Martin Luther Jr. *The Autobiography of Martin Luther King Jr.* New York: Warner Books, 1998.

Lake, Stuart N. *Wyatt Earp, Frontier Marshall.* New York: Pocket Books, 1994.

Levinson, Leonard Louis, ed. *Bartlett's Unfamiliar Quotations.* Chicago: Cowles Book Company, 1971.

London, Jack. *Letters from Jack London.* Edited by King Hendricks and Irving Shepard. New York: Odyssey, 1965.

Lowenstein, Roger. *Buffett: The Making of an American Capitalist.* New York: Random House, 1995.

Martz, L. "A Pair for the Court." *Newsweek* 107 (June 30, 1986):20-1.

Marx, Arthur. *My Life with Groucho: A Son's Eye View.* London: Robson Books, 1988.

Mencken, H. L., ed. *New Dictionary of Quotations on Historical Principles From Ancient and Modern Sources.* New York: Knopf, 1942.

Meyers, Jeffrey. *Gary Cooper: American Hero.* New York: Morrow, 1998.

Miller, Arthur. *Timebends: A Life.* New York: Grove Press, 1987.

Miner, Margaret and Hugh Rawson, eds. *American Heritage Dictionary of American Quotations.* New York: Penguin Reference, 1996.

Moen, Lynn and Judy Laik, eds. *Around the Circle Gently.* Berkeley, CA: Celestial Art, 1995.

Mosley, Leonard. *Disney's World: A Biography.* New York: Stein and Day, 1985.

Mosley, Leonard. *Lindbergh: A Biography.* Garden City, NY: Doubleday, 1976.

Mullane, Deirdre, ed. *Words to Make My Dream Children Live: A Book of African-American Quotations.* New York: Anchor Books, 1995.

Nixon, Richard. *The Memoirs of Richard Nixon.* New York: Grosset & Dunlap, 1978.

Oates, Stephen B. *Let the Trumpet Sound: The Life of Martin Luther King Jr.* New York: Harper & Row, 1987.

Pasquariello, Ronald D., ed. *Almanac of Quotable Quotes from 1990.* Englewood Cliffs, NJ: Prentice Hall, 1991.

Pepper, Frank S., ed. *The Wit and Wisdom of the 20th Century: A Dictionary of Quotations.* New York: P. Bedrick Books, 1987.

Plimpton, George, ed. *Writers at Work: Second Series.* New York: Penguin Books, 1963.

"Points to Ponder," *Reader's Digest* (August 1970):126.

Princeton Language Institute, ed. *21st Century Dictionary of Quotations.* New York: Dell Publishing, 1993.

Quindlen, Anna. *Living Out Loud.* New York: Random House, 1988.

Reader's Digest, ed. *Reader's Digest Quotable Quotes: Wit and Wisdom for All Occasions From America's Most Popular Magazine.* Pleasantville, NY: Reader's Digest Press, 1997.

Reader's Digest, ed. *Reader's Digest Treasury of Modern Quotes.* Pleasantville, NY: Reader's Digest Press, 1975.

FATHERHOOD

Reagan, Ronald. *The Wisdom & Humour of the Great Communicator*. San Francisco: Collins Publishers, 1995.

Riley, Dorothy Winbush, ed. *My Soul Looks Back, 'Less I Forget*. New York: Harper Collins, 1993.

Robinson, Sharon. *Stealing Home*. New York: Harper Collins, 1996.

"Rock On." *People* 48, no. 2 (July 14, 1997):133.

Rockefeller, John D. III. Speech at Family of Man awards dinner, October 1968, as quoted in "We Need Our Young Activists," *Reader's Digest* (August 1970):53-57.

Rogers, Fred and Barry Head. *Mister Rogers Talks with Parents*. New York: Berkley Books, 1983.

Roosevelt, Theodore. *Theodore Roosevelt's Letters to His Children*. New York: C. Scribner's Sons, 1919.

Sandburg, Carl. *The Letters of Carl Sandburg*. New York: Harcourt, Brace & World, 1968.

Schickel, Richard. *Clint Eastwood: A Biography*. New York: Knopf, 1996.

Sherline, Reid, ed. *Love Anyhow: Famous Fathers Write to Their Children*. New York: Timken Publishers, 1994.

Simpson, James Beasley, ed. *Simpson's Contemporary Quotations*. Boston: Houghton, Mifflin, 1988.

Spock, Benjamin and Steven J.Y. Parker. *Dr. Spock's Baby and Child Care*. New York: Pocket Books, 1998.

Stevenson, Burton Egbert, ed. *Home Book of Quotations*. New York: Dodd, Mead, 1967.

Stewart, Meiji, ed. *Parenting: Part Joy, Part Guerrilla Warfare*. Del Mar, CA: Keep Coming Back Company, 1997.

Toffler, Alvin. *Future Shock*. New York: Random House, 1970.

Tripp, Rhoda Thomas, ed. *International Thesaurus of Quotations*. New York: Thomas Y. Crowell, 1970.

Truman, Margaret. *Letters From Father*. New York: Arbor House, 1981.

Twain, Mark. *Mark Twain's Book for Bad Boys & Girls*. Chicago: Contemporary Books, 1995.

Updike, John. *Assorted Prose*. New York: Knopf, 1965.

Walton, Sam and John Huey. *Sam Walton, Made in America: My Story*. New York: Doubleday, 1992.

Washington Post, January 25, 1993, Sec. A, p. 11, col.1.

Watson, Thomas J. Jr. *Father, Son & Co.: My Life at IBM and Beyond*. New York: Bantam, 1990.

Webster's Dictionary of Quotations. New York: Smithmark, 1995.

Weiser, Marjorie P.K., ed. *Pegs to Hang Ideas On: A Book of Quotations*. New York: Evans, 1973.

Weiss, Irving and Anne D. Weiss, eds. *Reflections on Childhood: A Quotations Dictionary*. Santa Barbara, CA: ABC-CLIO, 1991.

West, Bob, ed. *Loving Children: Words of Love About Kids From Those Who Cherish Them*. San Francisco: Halo Books, 1993.

Williams, William Carlos. *The Selected Letters of William Carlos Williams*. Edited with an introduction by John C. Thirwall. New York: McDowell, Osolensky, 1957.

Winokur, Jon, ed. *Fathers*. New York: Plume, 1994.

Winokur, Jon, ed. *Friendly Advice*. New York: Penguin Books, 1990.

Woods, Earl. *Training a Tiger: A Father's Guide to Raising a Winner in Both Golf and Life*. New York: Harper Collins, 1997.

Wright, John Lloyd. *My Father Who Is on Earth*. New York: Putnam, 1962.

Young, Andrew. *A Way Out of No Way*. Nashville: Thomas Nelson, 1994.

Zall, Paul M., ed. *The Wit & Wisdom of the Founding Fathers*. Hopwell, NJ: Ecco Press, 1996.

Zappa, Frank and Peter Occhiogrosso. *The Real Frank Zappa Book*. New York: Poseidon Press, 1989.